19 poems

Sophia Carter

BookLeaf Publishing

India | USA | UK

Presentation by *BookLeaf Publishing*

Web: www.bookleafpub.com

E-mail: info@bookleafpub.com

ISBN: 9789358313574

First edition 2024

to my family

ACKNOWLEDGEMENT

Thankful for every experience!

Moment

A bird cries somewhere
warm coffee in a cold dawn
dense fog around me

Dream

Following the teachings
Of a not so ancient book,
I got to leave my body
and wander above.

I floated over myself.
 Lying in bed I looked,
 peacefully dead.
I adventured ahead.

There were some dreamy creatures,
neon lights, all kinds of shapes.
Others were nightmarish, those,
frightened me to death.

I grew tired of the journey,
turned back to bed.
Shadows had covered my body,
It was a horrid sight.

I wrapped my hand
around the silvery cord,
and yanked, and yanked, and yanked
Till my body was, again, mine.

Perspective

Watching the garden
From across the street I thought,
it now looked better

Smile

You told HER
all I wanted to hear.
With every text I saw,
my world disappear.

the ugliness hidden
Behind a smile.
You pretended to care.
I first saw your guile.

Gifts, work dinners,
you blatantly lied,
I would let you go,
holding back a cry

I could not believe,
yet another nightmare,
was becoming true:
You had an affair.

Rant

All look like Hellenics
Eat the transgenics
Struggle to be authentic
Forget the eugenics
Ban plastics
It's saprogenic
All this talk about ethnics
Selfishness is pathogenic
We're all schizophrenics
It's a pandemic

Let go

I prayed to God,
And the Devil,
even made a voodoo doll.
You didn't come back.
It was time to let you go.

Abandoned

One more abandoned dog
at the shelter,
already at capacity.
What to do?
His eyes have
that puzzled look.
He doesn't know
what's going on.
He must be feeling lost.

Where am I?
He wonders.
Then curls in a cage,
and he waits,
and he waits,
and he waits.

When are you coming back?
He cries all day,
 for days.
He falls deeper and deeper.
Despair turns into depression.

Ran out of tears,
food has no taste.

"I hate both humans and dogs"

The will to live now gone,
that puppy you once loved,
Is now the sad,
Abandoned dog
waiting to be euthanized.

Nana

wet lick on my face,
an overjoyed wagging tail,
always miss you friend

Fear

Rain drenched clothes,
cold bones and muddy feet,
our whole body hurt
running down the street.

We secretly loathed them.
In fear of persecution,
tongues and hands tied,
we mourned our illusions

Living in a cage we learned
how to fly in our dreams,
and swallow the words
we wanted to scream.

We obeyed our masters,
offered them our youth,
the future felt condemned,
but we knew the truth.

They couldn't steal the freedom
we carried within.
We had to push forward.
Fuck the agents of the regime!

Sea

cold salty sea breeze
murmuring secrets to me
 goosebumps on my skin

Cyan

12

Infinite blue sky,
bright burning light piercing through,
humans are so small

Darkness

I saw the shadow people,
in the fire light.
Later that night,
they entered mi mind,
took off their hats,
and offered a pact.
They would get off my path,
and remain hidden,
for as long as I'm hagridden.
I now live in fear,
of closing my eyes.

Mom

The soft scent of milk
that lingered after a hug.
How I shivered in fear,
when you called my name.
Memories of you

 Lost in a whirlwind
of your own creation,
you couldn't see me,
reaching for you
in desperation

I became a friend,
an allied, a nurse,
a counselor and a life coach;
Trying to haul you
Out of that hole.

I lost,
I lost YOU,
and ME
and all.
I gave up.

ABC Math

Today, we're learning to multiply
tap, tap, tap, tap, tap
using distributive property of multiplication.
tap, tap, tap, tap, tap
A, stop!
To multiply 3x23,
Humm hummm auuuhhh
B, be quiet! C, go to the restroom.
-"she's taking my pencils!"
-give back her pencils, D!
Where was I?
Ahh, 3x24, no 23
We break apart…
E, stop drawing and pay attention!
We break apart the 23
Into…sit down F!
We break apart the 24, no 23, into tens and ones,
How many tens are in 23?
20, 2, 1,
-I need to sharpen my pencil-,
-Ok, hurry up-,
So, there are 2 tens in 23 right?
How many ones?
4, great! So we can break 23 into 2 tens and 4
ones.

G! Open your book!
H, please go knock on the restroom door,
See what's taking C so long.
So, ok, using the distributive property of
multiplication,
I can say that …. J stop playing with K's hair!
Uhh, two times, no three times … L, put your
hand down.
3x24=(3x20)+(3x4) M, go back to your seat and
leave N alone!
Yes O? My head hurts- mine too, I say, mine too.
P, Q, please take O to the nurse.
Thumbs up if you're following…
So, 3x24=(3x20)+(3x4)
R, S start fighting…
STOP and seat down!
Wow, let me call the front office.
T, U, write whoever speaks while I'm on the
phone!
Ring, ring, ring, ring, ring, ring
No answer,
V, W please go find the Dean.
So, finally
How much is 3x23?
24? Thank you X
How much is 2x23?
Y…Z…. Breathe!

Legate

Gentle soul,
the wind still carries your voice.
A spot on the couch,
Still warm.

A Soft kiss on my nose
wakes me up.
Must be you who
curls at my feet in the dark.

The pain of a memory
brings you back,
at dusk only,
to be gone at dawn.

purr, purr, purr
I can hear you
from the other side.
Thank you for your visit,
come again tonight.

Farewell

You wore my favorite
Squared flannel shirt.
The one I used to wear
 after sex.

gloomy eyes and a stiff smile,
to complement.
Everything is …
Not ok.

One last embrace,
One last kiss,
Coupled with tears,
A last handwave.

I could taste the fear,
On your lips.
 We'll never meet again,
Your hands said.

See you soon we said.
Love can't ride high winds,
with crystal wings.
Farewell

Air

Shrouded in darkness,
the battle was fought
and lost,
time and time again.

A human carcass,
devoid of feelings.
Unable to harness
my scattered soul.

Last night,
the darkest one,
I cried myself to sleep,
one more time.

By the break of dawn,
the remains of us
were swept away,
and I could breathe again.
-

First love

For all that talk
Brings very little happiness
That first love,
Once is enough.

It's quite the turmoil,
Hyperbolic, violent, hungry,
That first love,
Once is enough.

It paints the world anew
And then it takes it all,
That first love,
Once is enough.

Teaches you how to fly,
Only to make you crash,
That first love
ONCE IS ENOUGH

Life

BREATHE
BREATHE
BREATHE
Breathe
Breathe
Breathe
BREATHE
BREATHE
BREATHE

www.ingramcontent.com/pod-product-compliance
Lightning Source LLC
LaVergne TN
LVHW041300200726
843507LV00014B/3062